5/29/18

Discovering Titanic's Remains

by Meish Goldish

Consultant: Melinda E. Ratchford, EdD
Titanic Historian and Associate Professor
Sister Christine Beck Department of Education
Belmont Abbey College
Belmont, North Carolina

BEARPORT
PUBLISHING

New York, New York

Credits

Cover, Titanic Painting © Ken Marschall; 4, © EMORY KRISTOF/National Geographic Creative; 5T, Bernard Walker/tinyurl.com/ycp77r6r/public domain; 5B, © Adam Jahiel; 6, The Design Lab; 7T, © Everett Historical/Shutterstock.com; 7B, Captain W. F. Wood/tinyurl.com/y7d2ceo7/public domain; 8–9, Titanic Painting © Ken Marschall; 9TR, © Everett Historical/Shutterstock.com; 9BR, © Sunphol Sorakul/Getty Images; 10, © Robosea/Cover Images/Newscom; 11, National Archives/tinyurl.com/ybkkuhxd/public domain; 12, © EMORY KRISTOF/National Geographic Creative; 13, © EMORY KRISTOF/National Geographic Creative; 14, © Susan Pease/Alamy Stock Photo; 15T, Photo Courtesy of Woods Hole Oceanographic Institution Archives; 15B, Photo Courtesy of Woods Hole Oceanographic Institution Archives; 16TL, © Igokapil/Dreamstime; 16TC, © Adam Jahiel; 16TR, © EMORY KRISTOF/National Geographic Creative; 16B, © Igokapil/Dreamstime; 17, NOAA/Institute for Exploration/University of Rhode Island or NOAA/IFE/URI; 18T, © EMORY KRISTOF/National Geographic Creative; 18B, Photo Courtesy of Woods Hole Oceanographic Institution Archives; 19T, © Science History Images/Alamy Stock Photo; 19B, © AP Photo/Jim MacMillan; 20T, © BRIAN HARRIS/Alamy Stock Photo; 20B, © BRIAN HARRIS/Alamy Stock Photo; 21T, © EMORY KRISTOF/National Geographic Creative; 21B, © EMORY KRISTOF/National Geographic Creative; 22TL, © Photo by Michel Boutefeu/Getty Images; 22BL, © Patrick Landmann/Science Source; 22TR, © Patrick Landmann/Science Source; 22BR, © Patrick Landmann/Science Source; 23L, © Photo by Peter Macdiarmid/Getty Images; 23R, © Peter Muhly/Alamy Stock Photo; 24L, © Dorling Kindersley Universal Images Group/Newscom; 24TR, Titanic Painting © Ken Marschall; 24BR, Titanic Painting © Ken Marschall; 25, Titanic Painting © Ken Marschall; 26–27, Titanic Painting © Ken Marschall; 28T, © THOMAS KLEINDINST/KRT/Newscom; 28BL, © JOSEPH H. BAILEY/National Geographic Creative; 28BR, Photo Courtesy of Woods Hole Oceanographic Institution Archives; 29T, Photo Courtesy of Woods Hole Oceanographic Institution Archives; 29BL, Photo Courtesy of Woods Hole Oceanographic Institution Archives; 29BR, © Photo by Michel Boutefeu/Getty Images; 31, © Science Museum/SSPL/The Image Works; 32, © Everett Historical/Shutterstock.com.

Publisher: Kenn Goin
Creative Director: Spencer Brinker
Photo Research: Editorial Directions, Inc.

Library of Congress Cataloging-in-Publication Data

Names: Goldish, Meish, author.
Title: Discovering Titanic's remains / by Meish Goldish.
Description: New York, New York : Bearport Publishing Company, [2018] |
  Series: Titanica | Includes bibliographical references and index.
Identifiers: LCCN 2017042962 (print) | LCCN 2017050872 (ebook) |
ISBN 9781684024926 (Ebook) | ISBN 9781684024346 (library)
Subjects: LCSH: Titanic (Steamship)—Juvenile literature. | Shipwrecks—North
  Atlantic Ocean—Juvenile literature.
Classification: LCC G530.T6 (ebook) | LCC G530.T6 G658 2018 (print) | DDC
  910.9163/4—dc23
LC record available at https://lccn.loc.gov/2017042962

For more information, write to Bearport Publishing Company, Inc., 45 West 21st Street, Suite 3B, New York, New York 10011. Printed in the United States of America.

10 9 8 7 6 5 4 3 2 1

CONTENTS

73 YEARS EARLIER

Deep-sea explorer Dr. Robert Ballard was losing hope. He had been sailing the Atlantic Ocean for more than a week, searching for the sunken remains of the *Titanic*. From their ship, Ballard and his crew guided an underwater camera along the ocean floor. Day after day, they saw only a dark, rocky ocean bottom on their **video** screens. There was no sign of the lost ship.

Dr. Robert Ballard (arms crossed) and his crew watch video screens showing the ocean floor.

Then, at around 2:00 AM on September 1, 1985, a giant object came into view on their screens. It was a **boiler** from the *Titanic*! It was the first object from the ship ever found since its sinking 73 years earlier.

The *Titanic* had 29 boilers. As the ship sank, five of them broke loose and spread across the ocean floor.

Ballard's crew compared the boiler they saw on the ocean floor with photos of the *Titanic*'s boilers to make sure they matched.

When they found the boiler, Ballard said, "Our first reaction was celebration. But then we realized that we were at a cemetery. We started seeing where the bodies had landed."

A Sinking Ship

The sinking of the *Titanic* was an unbelievable **tragedy**. On April 10, 1912, the new ship set sail on its first voyage, from England to New York. More than 2,200 passengers and crew were on board. Many people believed the modern **design** of the giant **ocean liner** made the ship unsinkable.

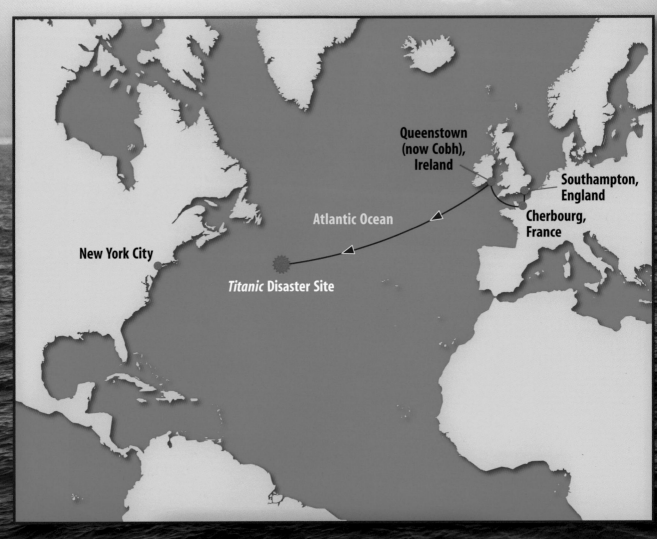

After leaving England, the *Titanic* made stops in France and Ireland before heading to New York.

Just before midnight on April 14, however, the *Titanic* struck an iceberg that tore holes in its side. Water rushed into the ship and began to weigh it down. Less than three hours later, the *Titanic* sank in very deep water. Only 705 people survived the disaster by escaping in lifeboats. More than 1,500 others drowned in the freezing ocean.

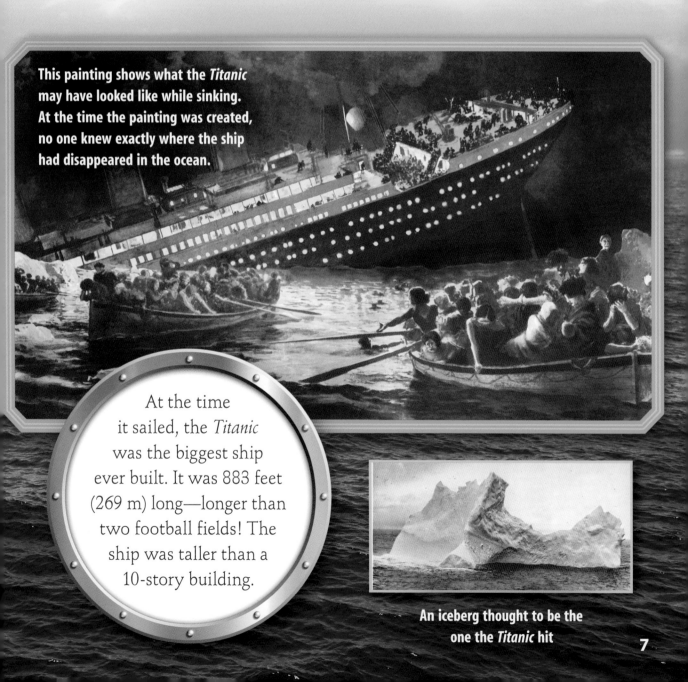

This painting shows what the *Titanic* may have looked like while sinking. At the time the painting was created, no one knew exactly where the ship had disappeared in the ocean.

At the time it sailed, the *Titanic* was the biggest ship ever built. It was 883 feet (269 m) long—longer than two football fields! The ship was taller than a 10-story building.

An iceberg thought to be the one the *Titanic* hit

DEEP AND DARK

Soon after the *Titanic* sank, people hoped it could be **recovered**. The job was impossible, however. The *Titanic* had sunk 12,460 feet (3,798 m) or almost 2 ½ miles (3.8 km) below the ocean's **surface**.

An artist's idea of what the sunken ship might look like

Even if it had been possible to reach the sunken ship, no one really knew where it was. Richie Kohler, a deep-sea diver, described what searching for the ship would be like in the deep ocean's darkness: "Imagine you drop an earring in your living room. Now you want to find it. And the way you have to do it is with all the lights out, and you can only use one eye and a small penlight."

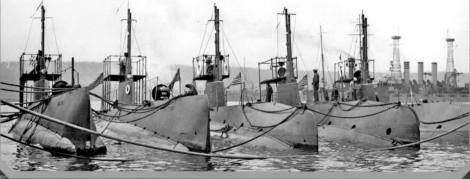

In 1912, submarines weren't able to travel much deeper than 200 feet (61 m) below the ocean's surface.

Most deep-sea divers can swim down to about 130 feet (40 m) before the pressure from the water above becomes too great for them. The *Titanic* sank almost 100 times deeper than that!

Sunlight never reaches the deepest parts of the ocean. In fact, depths greater than 3,280 feet (1,000 m) are known as the midnight zone.

A Gigantic Ocean to Search

More than 60 years passed without any sign of the *Titanic*. No remains floated to the ocean's surface to hint at the location of the ship. People feared the *Titanic* was lost forever. Then, in the late 1970s, scientists invented video cameras that worked more than 12,000 feet (3,658 m) underwater. They could be operated by **remote control** from a ship.

Underwater video cameras must be built tight enough to keep out water. They must also have bright lights to light up the dark ocean.

In 1977, teams of explorers used the cameras to search for the *Titanic*. Yet the ocean was gigantic. Where should they look? The searchers had a few clues. They knew the *Titanic*'s last reported location before it sank. They also knew the location from which the survivors had been rescued. Even with this information, no one could find the sunken ship for eight years.

In the 1970s, explorers didn't know that the *Titanic* had sunk more than 13 miles (21 km) from its last reported location.

Explorers used the location of *Titanic*'s survivors, such as those seen here, to estimate where the ship sank in the ocean.

A New Plan

In 1985, Ballard was ready to conduct his own search for the *Titanic*. He decided to work in a different way than earlier explorers. They had tried to find the ship itself. Ballard believed it would be smarter to search instead for the field of **debris**—the items that fell from the *Titanic* as it sank.

Ballard knew that thousands of items from the *Titanic*, like those seen here, had spread across the ocean floor.

"A long trail of objects would have scattered out of the ship as she plunged to the bottom," he said. "And because the trail would cover a wider area than the ship itself, it would be easier to find." Ballard figured that once debris was discovered, it would lead to the actual ship.

Ballard used the speed and direction of the ocean **currents** on the night the *Titanic* sank to estimate how far debris might have scattered in the water.

LIGHTS, CAMERAS, EXPLORE!

On August 22, 1985, Ballard and his crew began to explore. They sailed on a U.S. Navy ship called the *Knorr*. They were joined by French explorers led by Jean-Louis Michel. The two groups had special equipment on board to study the ocean. Most important was *Argo*. It was an **unmanned** deep-sea submarine that Ballard had designed himself.

The research ship *Knorr*

Argo traveled more than 12,000 feet (3,658 m) below the ocean's surface. Crew members on the *Knorr* carefully guided its movements. *Argo*'s cameras took video of the ocean floor. The explorers viewed the images on screens aboard the ship. After the search area was widened to look for debris, *Argo* spotted *Titanic*'s boiler. Ballard's plan had worked!

Besides having video cameras, *Argo* had built-in **sonar** that could search the sea floor for small pieces of debris.

Argo was pulled along the ocean floor by a cable attached to the *Knorr*.

Ballard's crew used a second unmanned submarine, called ANGUS, to take thousands of photographs of the ocean floor.

FINDING MORE

After finding *Titanic*'s boiler, *Argo*'s cameras spotted more remains. They included chairs, cups, dishes, clothing, jewelry, and shoes. There was even a case filled with unbroken perfume bottles! Later, it was learned that the case belonged to a perfume maker who probably had planned to sell the bottles to stores after he arrived in New York.

A *Titanic* passenger was probably wearing these shoes as the ship sank.

These china plates did not break when the ship hit the ocean floor.

This piece of a bench was once on the deck of the *Titanic*.

This bathtub came to rest on the ocean floor.

Titanic's field of debris stretched nearly 2,000 feet (610 m)— the length of almost six football fields!

As Ballard had predicted, the trail of debris led to the ship itself. Soon, *Argo* located *Titanic's* **hull**. It also found the ship's **bow** and **stern**. They lay on the ocean floor in two separate pieces—1,970 feet (600 m) apart—facing in opposite directions! Thick layers of **rust** covered much of the ship.

A part of the *Titanic*, heavily covered with rust

A Look Inside

After viewing the remains for four days, Ballard and his crew had to leave the site due to stormy seas. More than ten months later, in July 1986, the team returned to further examine the ship. They made history again. For the first time ever, the explorers rode down to the sunken ship in a small submarine called *Alvin*. "We could barely control our excitement as the ship unfolded beneath us," Ballard said.

Ballard and his crew inside *Alvin*

The submarine *Alvin*

The explorers were amazed. They could see the ship's damaged Grand Staircase close up. A glass **chandelier** still hung from the ceiling! However, Ballard was surprised when he went to view the ship's wooden **deck**. Most of it had been **devoured** by millions of wood-eating worms.

Ballard found no human remains while examining the ship. At one point, he thought he saw a human head in the sand. It turned out to be a child's doll.

Titanic's **Grand Staircase, as it looked before the ship sank**

Ballard and his crew used a remote-controlled robot named *Jason Junior*, or JJ, to take photographs of the ship's insides.

TWO OPINIONS

Before leaving the ship's ruins, Ballard placed two signs on the *Titanic*. One honored those who had died. The other asked that the ship be left alone. Ballard believed that items from the sunken ship should not be taken out of the ocean. Many people agreed with him, including families of the drowned **victims**. They felt the remains were in a **sacred** graveyard.

In the 1980s, *Titanic* survivor Eva Hart (left), who had been seven years old (above) when the ship sailed, came out against removing remains. "The ship is its own memorial," she said. "Leave it there."

Other people disagreed. They argued that *Titanic*'s remains had historical importance. They wanted to **salvage** everything possible from the ship before it completely **disintegrated**. Since *Titanic*'s location was now known, the question arose: Should future explorers be allowed to remove *Titanic*'s remains from the ocean?

One of the signs Dr. Ballard left on the ship's ruins

Over the years, salt water has destroyed parts of the ship.

Ballard contacted the 24 remaining survivors of the *Titanic*, plus various museums around the world. He reported, "There wasn't a single person or organization in favor of recovering **artifacts**."

REMOVING REMAINS

In 1987, the U.S. government allowed an Atlanta, Georgia, company called RMS Titanic to salvage *Titanic*'s remains. Since then, the company has brought up more than 6,000 artifacts from the ocean. A U.S. court ruled that none of the items RMS Titanic retrieved may be sold. They can only be displayed in museums and other places around the world.

Titanic remains are on display in museums around the world. Many of the items have been cleaned and repaired.

Because the *Titanic* sank in **international waters**, the ship's remains do not belong to any country.

However, other explorers have been allowed to sell remains that they took from the ocean. At one **auction** in New York, a buyer paid $56,250 for an original ticket on the *Titanic* voyage. In 2015, another person paid $120,000 for a menu from one of the *Titanic*'s restaurants. A printed message that read, "We have struck an iceberg," sent from the ship's **telegraph** sold for $27,500.

In 2012, a museum opened in Belfast, Northern Ireland, where the *Titanic* was built. Visitors can see exactly where the ship was constructed and where it sailed from.

The violin used by Wallace Hartley, the *Titanic's* band leader, was purchased in 2013 for 1.7 million dollars.

LESSONS LEARNED

The discovery of *Titanic* taught historians much about the famous ship. However, finding its remains also **disproved** some beliefs about the tragic event. For example, many people had thought that the giant ship sank in one piece. However, photographs of the separated bow and stern prove that the ship split in two as it sank.

As *Titanic*'s bow sank, the stern rose out of the water and into the air. The pressure it put on the hull became so great that the ship broke apart.

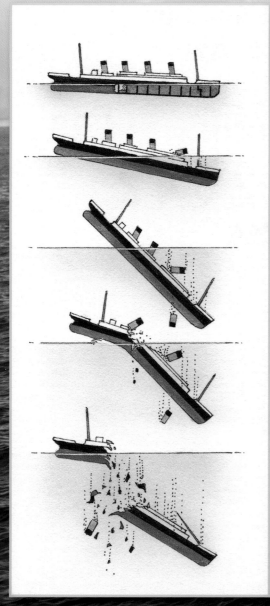

The bow, or front of the ship (top), and the stern, or back (bottom), lay apart on the ocean floor.

People had also thought the *Titanic* flooded because the iceberg punched a giant 300-foot (91 m) long hole in its side. However, explorers later found that the iceberg made just six small gashes in the ship's hull. Water rushed into the gashes and flooded 6 of the 16 watertight compartments. Eventually, the weight of the floodwater sank the ship.

Scientists discovered that the quality of the steel used to build the *Titanic* was not strong enough to stand up to the ocean's freezing water. As a result, the hull's metal plates broke off when the water pushed against them.

This painting shows how an iceberg may have damaged the *Titanic*'s hull.

TITANIC'S FUTURE

What has become of *Titanic*'s remains that still lie on the ocean floor? In 2004, Ballard and his crew returned to the wreck site to find out. They were saddened by what they found. Ballard wrote, "We could see where explorers' submarines had landed, where they had crushed the floors, where they had pulled fixtures off the ship, plus all the garbage they had left behind."

Starting in 2018, people can ride in a submarine to visit the *Titanic* wreck site. The eight-day tour, run by a British company, will cost each passenger $105,000!

Today, explorers aren't the only problem. Nature is also damaging the *Titanic*. Worms and **bacteria** continue to eat away at the wood. Other tiny sea creatures eat the iron. Many scientists believe the ship will completely disappear by 2030.

Over the years, people have proposed many interesting ideas to save the *Titanic* from the sea. Soon after it sank, someone suggested using giant magnets to pull the ship up to the water's surface. Another idea was to fill the sunken wreck with ping-pong balls to help it float to the surface.

EXPLORERS' EQUIPMENT

The explorers who discovered and examined *Titanic*'s remains needed special equipment to do their work. Here is some of the technology they used.

In 1985, Ballard and his crew worked from the U.S. Navy ship *Knorr*. It had a positioning system that tracked the *Titanic*'s exact location in the ocean at all times.

Argo was an unmanned vehicle that carried video cameras and sonar. Equipped with powerful lights, it could travel to a depth of 20,000 feet (6,096 m) in the dark ocean waters.

ANGUS was an unmanned vehicle built to travel along the rocky ocean floor. Protected by a heavy steel frame, its cameras took thousands of color photographs of *Titanic*'s remains.

In 1986, *Alvin* became the first manned submarine to carry explorers to *Titanic*'s remains. It was equipped with four video cameras.

Jason Junior, or *JJ*, was a remote-controlled robot equipped with cameras that took photographs of the remains. *JJ* explored places inside the *Titanic* that *Alvin* could not fit into.

In 1987, French explorers rode inside the submarine *Nautile* to collect the first remains of the *Titanic*. It had two robotic arms to pick items off the ocean floor.

GLOSSARY

artifacts (ART-uh-fakts) objects of historical interest that were made by people

auction (AWK-shuhn) a sale where something is sold to the person who offers the highest price

bacteria (bac-TIHR-ee-uh) tiny life-forms that can be seen only under a microscope

boiler (BOI-lur) a tank that burns fuel in order to heat or power a building or other structure, such as a ship

bow (BOU) the front end of a ship

chandelier (shan-duh-LIHR) a fancy light fixture that hangs from the ceiling

currents (KUR-uhnts) the movements of water in an ocean or river

debris (duh-BREE) pieces of something that has been destroyed

deck (DEK) the floor of a ship or boat

design (di-ZINE) the look of something that has been built

devoured (di-VOURD) destroyed; eaten hungrily

disintegrated (diss-IN-tuh-gray-tid) broke into small pieces

disproved (diss-PRUVD) to prove that something is untrue

hull (HUHL) the frame or body of a ship

international waters (in-tur-NASH-uh-nuhl WAH-turz) areas of the sea or ocean that are not under the control of any country

ocean liner (OH-shuhn LINE-ur) a large ship that can carry many people across the ocean

recovered (ri-KUHV-urd) gotten back after a loss

remote control (ri-MOHT kuhn-TROHL) a system for operating machines from a distance

rust (RUHST) the reddish-brown substance that can form on iron and steel when they are exposed to moisture and air

sacred (SAY-krid) holy, religious

salvage (SAL-vij) to rescue property from a shipwreck, fire, or any disaster

sonar (SOH-nar) technology that uses sound to locate objects underwater

stern (STERN) the rear or back of a ship

surface (SUR-fiss) the top layer of something, such as an ocean or river

telegraph (TELL-uh-graf) a way to send messages over long distances

tragedy (TRAJ-uh-dee) a sad and terrible event

unmanned (UN-mand) without a person inside

victims (VIK-tuhmz) people who are hurt or killed in an accident or disaster

video (VID-ee-oh) moving pictures that can be viewed on a television or computer screen

BIBLIOGRAPHY

Adams, Simon. *Titanic.* New York: Dorling Kindersley (2004).

Ballard, Dr. Robert D. *The Discovery of the Titanic.* New York: Warner (1988).

Ballard, Robert D., and Michael Sweeney. *Return to Titanic.* Washington, DC: National Geographic (2004).

Brewster, Hugh, and Ken Marschall. *Inside the Titanic.* Boston: Little, Brown (1997).

READ MORE

Ballard, Robert D. *Exploring the Titanic.* Toronto: Madison Press (2014).

Blake, Kevin. *Titanic's Fatal Voyage (Titanica).* New York: Bearport (2018).

Driscoll, Laura. *Titanic: The Story Lives On!* New York: Penguin (2012).

LEARN MORE ONLINE

To learn more about the *Titanic*'s remains, visit
www.bearportpublishing.com/Titanica

Index

About the Author

Meish Goldish has written more than 300 books for children. His book *Colonial Williamsburg* was named a Notable Social Studies Trade Book for Young People in 2017 by the National Council for the Social Studies and the Children's Book Council. He lives in Brooklyn, New York.